Spotlight on the 13 Colonies
Birth of a Nation

★ ★ ★ ★ ★ ★ ★ ★ ★ ★ ★ ★ ★

THE COLONY OF
MARYLAND

Cecily Jobes

PowerKiDS press™

NEW YORK

Published in 2016 by The Rosen Publishing Group, Inc.
29 East 21st Street, New York, NY 10010

Editor: Caitlin McAneney
Book Design: Andrea Davison-Bartolotta

Photo Credits: Cover, pp. 5, 12–13 (main) North Wind Picture Archive; p. 4 Jon Bilous/Shutterstock.com;
pp. 6–7 Acroterion/Wikimedia Commons; p. 9 SuperStock/Getty Images; pp. 10, 15 (inset) Courtesy of
Wikimedia Commons; p. 11 Archive Photos/Stringer/Getty Images; p. 13 (inset) Joseph Sohm/Shutterstock.com;
pp. 14, 15 (main) Courtesy of the Library of Congress; p. 15 (background) Iriana Shiyan/Shutterstock.com;
p. 16 Matanya/US Capitol/Wikimedia Commons; p. 17 (left) Courtesy of The New York Public Library Digital
Collections; p. 17 (right) Courtesy of the Maryland State Archives; p. 18 The White House Historical Association/
Wikimedia Commons; p. 19 Tom Williams/Roll Call/Getty Images; p. 21 Courtesy of U.S. Army Center of Military
History; p. 22 VectorPic/Shutterstock.com.

Cataloging-in-Publication Data

Jobes, Cecily.
The colony of Maryland / by Cecily Jobes.
p. cm. — (Spotlight on the 13 colonies: Birth of a nation)
Includes index.
ISBN 978-1-4994-0504-0 (pbk.)
ISBN 978-1-4994-0505-7 (6 pack)
ISBN 978-1-4994-0507-1 (library binding)
1. Maryland — History — Colonial period, ca. 1600-1775 — Juvenile literature. 2. Maryland — History —
1775-1865 — Juvenile literature. I. Title.
F184.J63 2016
975.2'02—d23

Manufactured in the United States of America

CPSIA Compliance Information: Batch #WS15PK: For further information contact Rosen Publishing, New York, New York at 1-800-237-9932.

Contents

Explorers on the Chesapeake

Maryland is a state on the northern Chesapeake Bay. Chesapeake Bay is an estuary, or a body of water near an ocean where salt water and freshwater meet. This region is full of beautiful nature and history. Before Maryland was a state, it was an American colony, and before that, it was home to many Native American tribes.

Around 12,000 years ago, the **ancestors** of Native Americans arrived in the area that's now Maryland. They developed ways to fish, hunt, grow food, and create art. In 1524, an Italian explorer named Giovanni da Verrazano sailed past the mouth of Chesapeake Bay. In 1572, the Spanish governor of Florida, Pedro Menéndez de Avilés, explored Chesapeake Bay.

English captain John Smith led the first major European expedition to Chesapeake Bay in 1608. Smith explored and charted nearly 3,000 miles (4,828 km) along the Chesapeake Bay and its **tributaries**. He told of beautiful lands and friendly natives, which sparked interest in trading in the area.

Maryland coastline

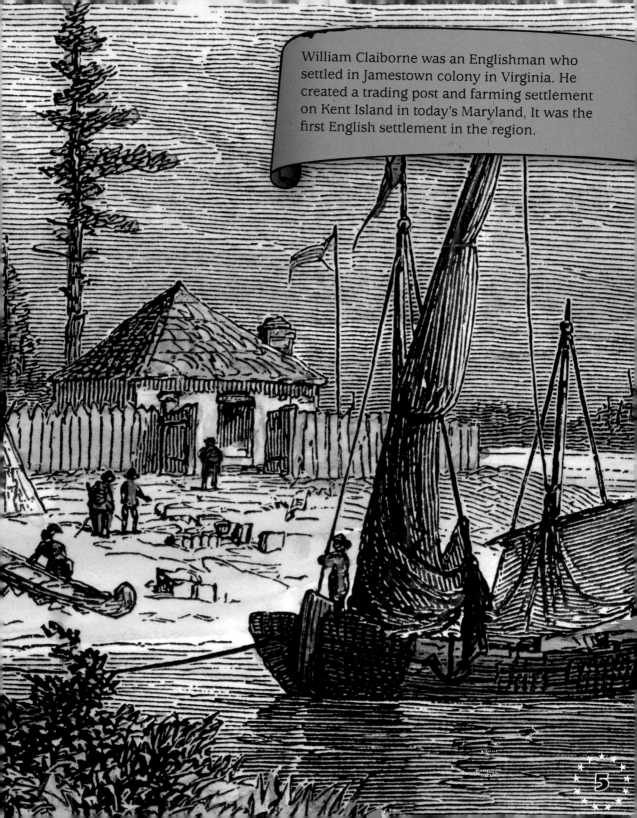

William Claiborne was an Englishman who settled in Jamestown colony in Virginia. He created a trading post and farming settlement on Kent Island in today's Maryland. It was the first English settlement in the region.

Lord Baltimore's Land

In the early 1600s, England wasn't a place of religious freedom. Those who weren't a part of the Church of England, including Catholics, had a hard time gaining wealth, respect, and rights in English society. Many colonies, such as Pennsylvania and Massachusetts, began out of the need for a place free from religious **persecution**.

George Calvert, given the title Lord Baltimore, was a Catholic who wanted to create a colony where other Catholics could find success. Calvert died before he could bring his colony into being. However, his son Cecilius Calvert took on the task. In 1632, England's King Charles I gave Lord Baltimore's family a **charter** for a colony in America. The colony was named Maryland after King Charles's wife, Henrietta Maria, who was Catholic.

Cecilius Calvert became the second Lord Baltimore. He sent nearly 140 settlers to the new colony of Maryland. Seventeen of the settlers were wealthy Catholic gentlemen. The rest were **indentured servants**, who were mainly Protestant.

On November 22, 1633, the settlers left England on two ships, the *Ark* and the *Dove*. They landed in March 1634 on St. Clement's Island. This is a replica of the *Dove*.

7

St. Mary's Settlement

Lord Baltimore's settlers named their settlement St. Mary's. At this time, there were about 40 Native American tribes in the area. The Yaocomaco tribe was already living near St. Mary's. The Yaocomaco were friendly and willing to trade.

The Yaocomaco taught settlers how to plant crops such as corn and beans. They were also willing to sell their land to settlers. The settlers paid them in cloth and metal tools. The settlers were even able to live in the Yaocomaco's longhouses, which were called *witchotts*.

Lord Baltimore controlled the colony from his home in England. He sent his brother, Leonard Calvert, to the colony as the first governor. In 1637, the colonists formed an assembly of representatives to give them a voice in colonial government. Maryland watered the seeds of **democracy** from its very beginning. The colonists couldn't be taxed without agreeing to it. They also had a say in which laws would govern them.

This painting shows colonists meeting a native tribe near their settlement at St. Mary's. The good relations between natives and colonists in Maryland were helpful for the colonists. Other colonies dealt with many years of **tension** with native tribes that often led to bloody fights.

Early Challenges

Colonists faced many challenges during Maryland's early years. Maryland's colonists risked death by illnesses, such as **malaria** and influenza, or the flu. Settlers didn't live long and often died in childhood.

People continued to move to Maryland, however. There was promise of success in business and farming. Many came for religious freedom. Maryland's colonists were granted religious freedom officially in 1649, when Lord Baltimore called for the Maryland Assembly to pass the Maryland Toleration Act.

The Maryland Toleration Act drew Puritans to the area. Puritans escaped England because they were persecuted for believing the Church of England should be rid of Catholic practices. Puritans had strong faith in God and were very firm about going to church. They founded the town of Annapolis and took part in Maryland's assembly. However, the Puritans gained so much power they overthrew St. Mary's and took control. The Puritans then did away with the Maryland Toleration Act.

Maryland Toleration Act

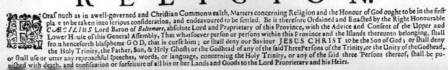

This picture depicts Puritans traveling on rough seas to get to America.

Maryland's Industries

Lord Baltimore regained control, but it lasted only until 1692, when Maryland became a royal colony. Meanwhile, Maryland's early industries, or businesses, were on the rise. Maryland's farmers produced wheat and corn, but the most important crop was tobacco. In the earliest days of the colony, indentured servants did the hard labor of farming. However, fewer indentured servants were arriving.

Slaves were brought to Maryland starting in the mid-1600s. Many slaves worked on large farms called plantations. They were forced to do backbreaking work for no pay. They were punished cruelly when they didn't obey. With slave labor, the tobacco crop boomed and Maryland's economy flourished. Famous slaves from Maryland include Josiah Henson and Frederick Douglass.

Maryland's location on Chesapeake Bay gave colonists access to the ocean. This made it a great place for trade. Maryland developed a successful shipbuilding industry because of its location on Chesapeake Bay. Ships were needed for trade, especially trade across the Atlantic Ocean.

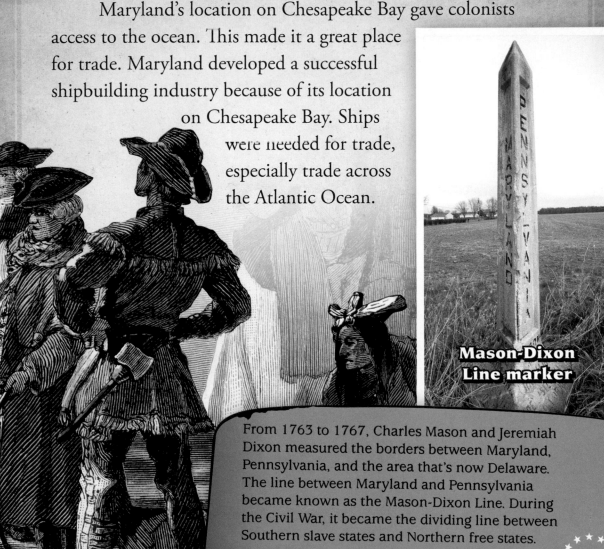

Mason-Dixon Line marker

From 1763 to 1767, Charles Mason and Jeremiah Dixon measured the borders between Maryland, Pennsylvania, and the area that's now Delaware. The line between Maryland and Pennsylvania became known as the Mason-Dixon Line. During the Civil War, it became the dividing line between Southern slave states and Northern free states.

Boycotting the British

By the mid-1700s, tension was starting to brew between the colonies and England. The colonists objected to the taxes England forced on them. England had its own reasons for raising colonial taxes. In 1754, the French and Indian War broke out between the British and French over American territory. England won the war, but still needed to pay for it. England also spent money paying for soldiers on the western frontier to keep peace between Native Americans and colonists.

Since the colonies were involved in these costs, England's King George III and **Parliament** thought it was fair to tax them. The Stamp Act of 1765 put a tax on paper products. Maryland was the first colony to **declare** it wouldn't pay the unfair tax. Colonists in Maryland opposed the act by **boycotting** stamps and protesting in Annapolis. The colonists felt it was unfair to pay taxes if they didn't have a say in Parliament.

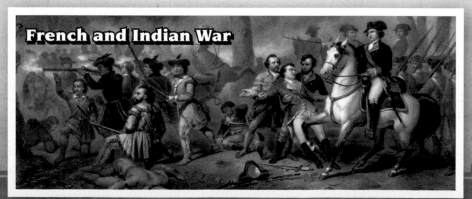

French and Indian War

Jonas Green was the publisher of the *Maryland Gazette*. On September 5, 1765, Green announced he would no longer publish the newspaper because the Stamp Act would tax it. In his last issue of the *Gazette*, he protested the Stamp Act by printing a skull and crossbones where the tax stamp should have gone.

skull and crossbones

Jonas Green house

Maryland's Patriots

In 1774, representatives from the colonies met in Philadelphia, Pennsylvania, in meetings that became known as the First Continental Congress. Colonial representatives discussed Britain's unfair taxes. Maryland's representatives included Samuel Chase, Robert Goldsborough, Thomas Johnson, William Paca, and Matthew Tilghman. The representatives wrote a **petition** to the king and organized a boycott. Patriots in Maryland joined the Continental Association, which aimed to harm British businesses. Patriots supported protests and boycotts. Some wanted the colonies to break from England.

Marylander Samuel Chase was a patriot who participated in the Continental Congress in 1774 and signed the Declaration of Independence in 1776. After the American Revolution, he served as a Supreme Court justice.

In October 1774, the *Peggy Stewart* sailed into Annapolis, Maryland. The ship, owned by Anthony Stewart, was full of British tea. This angered Maryland's patriots because they were boycotting British tea. On October 19, 1774, Stewart agreed to have his ship and tea burned out of fear of the patriots.

The boycotts and protests led to more British soldiers occupying the colonies. Tension increased until the first shot of the American Revolution was fired at Lexington, Massachusetts, on April 19, 1775.

burning of the *Peggy Stewart*

Samuel Chase

Fighting for Independence

The First Continental Congress helped unite the colonies against England's unfair rule. In May 1775, representatives from each colony met again in Philadelphia. Today, this is known as the Second Continental Congress. Maryland's representatives included Samuel Chase, William Paca, Thomas Stone, Charles Carroll, and others.

signing of the Declaration of Independence

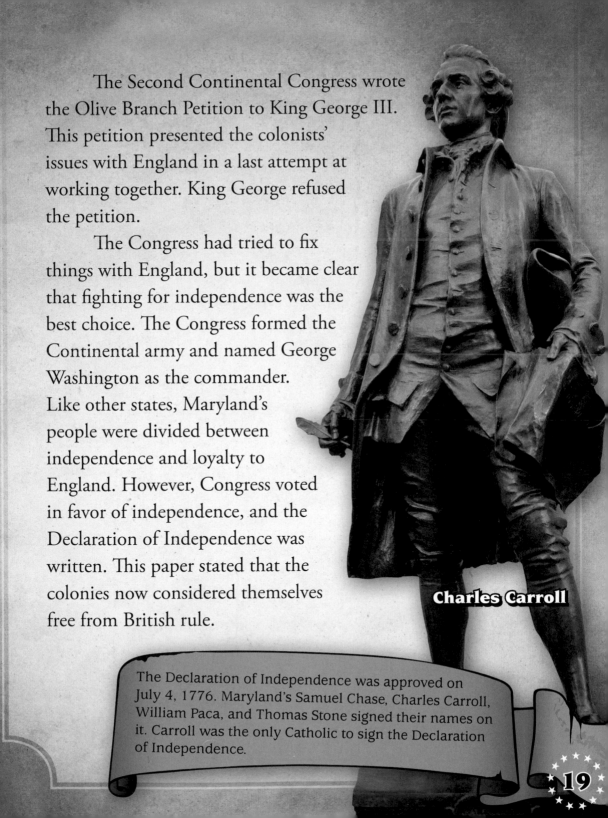

The Second Continental Congress wrote the Olive Branch Petition to King George III. This petition presented the colonists' issues with England in a last attempt at working together. King George refused the petition.

The Congress had tried to fix things with England, but it became clear that fighting for independence was the best choice. The Congress formed the Continental army and named George Washington as the commander. Like other states, Maryland's people were divided between independence and loyalty to England. However, Congress voted in favor of independence, and the Declaration of Independence was written. This paper stated that the colonies now considered themselves free from British rule.

Charles Carroll

The Declaration of Independence was approved on July 4, 1776. Maryland's Samuel Chase, Charles Carroll, William Paca, and Thomas Stone signed their names on it. Carroll was the only Catholic to sign the Declaration of Independence.

The Old Line

The colony-states—no longer British colonies, but not yet independent states—still had to win the war to be truly free. Their new army, made of mostly untrained soldiers, had to beat one of the greatest armies in the world. Luckily, Maryland's regiments, or troops, were organized, wore uniforms, and were well trained.

Marylanders fought at the first major battle of the American Revolution, the Battle of Long Island, on August 27, 1776. The Maryland regiment bravely defended the Continental army as it withdrew from the battle. The regiment became known as the "Old Line." That may be how Maryland got its nickname as the "Old Line State." Maryland also helped the war effort by paying for **privateers** to capture British ships.

No major battles were fought in Maryland. However, Baltimore was the location of the Continental Congress from December 1776 to February 1777. The Congress met in a house belonging to Henry Fite, which was called "Congress Hall."

This painting shows the 1st Maryland Regiment fighting in a line formation during the Battle of Guilford Courthouse, in what is today Greensboro, North Carolina, on March 15, 1781.

The State of Maryland

The American Revolution ended in 1781, when the British surrendered to the Continental army at Yorktown, Virginia. Maryland's own patriot Tench Tilghman carried the formal paper declaring America's victory from Yorktown to the Continental Congress in Philadelphia.

During the war, America had been governed by the Articles of Confederation. However, the Articles gave too much power to states and not enough to the federal government. State representatives met at the Annapolis Convention in Maryland in September 1786 to discuss easier trade between states. They also called for another convention to discuss ways to improve the Articles.

In May 1787, state representatives once again met in Philadelphia for meetings later known as the Constitutional Convention. This convention created a new **constitution** to govern the United States. Maryland became the seventh state to join the United States when it approved the Constitution on April 28, 1788. In 1790, some of Maryland's land became Washington, D.C., the capital of the United States.

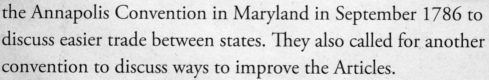

Glossary

ancestor: A person who comes before others in their family tree.

boycott: To refuse to buy something to protest a group or company.

charter: A piece of writing from a king or other leader that grants or guarantees something.

constitution: The basic rules by which a country or state is governed.

declare: To state something formally.

democracy: A government by the people.

indentured servant: A person who works for another person for a fixed amount of time for payment of travel or living costs.

malaria: A disease involving a high fever that's passed from one person to another by mosquito bites.

Parliament: The group in England that makes the country's laws.

persecution: The act of treating someone cruelly or unfairly especially because of race or beliefs.

petition: A formal way to ask for something to be done.

privateer: An armed private ship used by a government to fight enemy ships.

tension: A state of unrest or opposition between individuals or groups.

tributary: A stream that feeds into a larger stream or other body of water.

Index

Primary Source List

p. 10
Facsimile of a Broadside of the Maryland Toleration Act of 1649. Original created by Lord Baltimore and passed by the assembly of the province of Maryland. Ink on paper. Original printed 1649.

p. 15 (main)
Jonas Green House. Creator unknown. Part wood frame and part brick. Built in 1738. Now located at 124 Charles Street, Annapolis, MD.

p. 15 (inset)
The Maryland Gazette. Printed by Jonas Green. Newspaper. September 5, 1765.

Websites

Due to the changing nature of Internet links, PowerKids Press has developed an online list of websites related to the subject of this book. This site is updated regularly. Please use this link to access the list: www.powerkidslinks.com/s13c/mary